W9-CLY-020

811.54 W749i

Wilson, John, 1947-

Ink on paper

DATE DUE

NOV 1 6 2006			

DEMCO 38-297

COLUMBIA COLLEGE LIBRARY
600 S. MICHIGAN AVENUE
CHICAGO, IL 60605

ink on paper

Poems on

Chinese &

Japanese

Paintings

John Wilson

CITY LIGHTS BOOKS
SAN FRANCISCO

© 2001 by John Wilson

All rights reserved
10 9 8 7 6 5 4 3 2 1

Cover & book design: Stefan Gutermuth/doubleu-gee
Set in Guardi and Weiss

Cover painting: Anonymous, *Asleep in a Boat near the Shore* [Fl.916.537].
Reproduced by courtesy of the Freer Gallery of Art, Smithsonian Institution,
Washington D.C.

Library of Congress Cataloging-in-Publication Data

Wilson, John, 1947—
    Ink on Paper: poems on Chinese and Japanese paintings / John Wilson
        p.   cm.
    ISBN 0-87286-393-X
        1. Painting, Oriental—Poetry. 2. Asia—Poetry. I. Title

    PS3623.1585 155 2001
    811′ .54—dc21   20001042128

811.54 W749i

Wilson, John, 1947-

Ink on paper

CITY LIGHTS BOOKS are edited by Lawrence Ferlinghetti and Nancy J. Peters
and published at the City Lights Bookstore, 261 Columbus Avenue, San Francisco, CA 94133.
www.citylights.com.

Acknowledgments

Images of paintings in this book have been reproduced by courtesy
of the following museums, galleries, and individual owners:

Anonymous (late Ming Dynasty, 1368-1644):
Asleep in a Boat near the Shore.
Freer Gallery of Art, Smithsonian Institution, Washington, D.C.

Anonymous (T'ang Dynasty, 618-906):
Emperor Ming-huang's Journey to Shu.
National Palace Museum, Taipei, Taiwan, Republic of China.

Ku K'ai-chih (344-405), attribution: *Admonitions of the Court Instructress.*
British Museum, London, England.

Kusumi Morikage (ca. 1610 - ca. 1700): *Enjoying the Evening Cool.*
Tokyo National Museum, Tokyo, Japan.

Miyamoto Musashi, or Niten (1584-1645): *Shrike on a Bare Branch.*
Kubosō Memorial Art Museum, Izumi, Japan.

Mu-ch'i (fl. mid-13th century): *Persimmons.*
Ryōkōin, Daitokuji, Kyōto, Japan.

Sengai (1751-1837): *Enjoying the Evening Cool.*
Idemitsu Museum of Arts, Tokyo, Japan.
Solitary Life at Kyobaku-in.
Idemitsu Museum of Arts, Tokyo, Japan.

Sesshū (1420-1506): *Autumn and Winter Landscapes.*
Tokyo National Museum, Tokyo, Japan.

Sesson (fl.1542-1573): *Boat in a Storm.*
Nomura Museum of Arts, Kyōto, Japan.

Shih K'o (10th century): *Second Patriarch Harmonizing His Mind.*
Tokyo National Museum, Tokyo, Japan.

Tan-an (fl. ca. 1500): *Heron.*
Tokyo National Museum, Tokyo, Japan.

Yosa Buson (1716-1784): *Crows* (detail).
Kitamura Museum, Kyōto, Japan.
Night Snow over City (detail).
Haruta Muto, Kōbe, Japan.

Poems in this collection, some with different titles, have been published
in *Kansas Quarterly*, *Spectrum*, and the *Daily Nexus*.

The author would like to thank Diane Roby, Motoko Naruse, Bob
DeBris, Ryuji Tsuyuki, and Alan Stephens for their help and advice,
and the College of Creative Studies, UCSB, for a generous grant.

To JoAnne

TABLE OF CONTENTS

paintings

poems

ink *on paper*

Sesshū (1420-1506): *Autumn and Winter Landscapes* (Winter).
TOKYO NATIONAL MUSEUM, TOKYO, JAPAN.

I   Nine brush strokes make
     mankind

     walking
     toward Sesshū's

     cliff in mid-air
     turning

     with trees and rocks
     and flesh

     and mind to pure
     clearness.

     What good do whole
     nations

     beside
     this?

Sesson (fl.1542-1573): *Boat in a Storm*.
NOMURA MUSEUM OF ARTS, KYŌTO, JAPAN.

II   The women then
would be

under grass roofs
singing

over fish, kelp
and rice

as their minds moved
with what

we see outside:
Sesson's

boat in a storm.

Driven toward
the rocks

it lists,
its lines about

to snap;
the fishermen's

lives have somehow
shifted

to five sheer crests
breaking

toward the thatch,
bamboo

and leafless tree
on shore

almost breaking
like waves.

Everything strife,
nothing

unstrained,
even the roof

buckles
blasted by wind,

and yet
Sesson touched all

strangely
with a stillness.

We cannot hear
the song

or see
the strong singers

under their roof
singing.

Miyamoto Musashi, or Niten (1584-1645): *Shrike on a Bare Branch*.
KUBOSŌ MEMORIAL ART MUSEUM, IZUMI, JAPAN.

III His shrike
on a bare branch

is Musashi
himself,

the swordsman
none surpassed.

Thrust swordlike into
white

space
this slight branch cuts through

the world
that a few leaves

and one
stem of bamboo

compose
in a corner

down low
but without which

the branch
could never stand.

The shrike
impales its prey

on thorns,
a swordsman's bird!

Miyamoto's
fierce stroke

(in sword and brush)
strikes out

of the shrike's eye
as if

at the void
itself

it could swoop to
attack.

IV   Summer's mist must soften
       Sengai's contented man

       who sits unrobed outside
       to feel the evening breeze

       and must soften the reeds
       behind him and the bottle

       by his foot, which also
       softens the man whose mind

       is everything we see
       slightly blurred with pleasure

       at being simply there
       on a dock by a stream.

Sengai (1751-1837): *Enjoying the Evening Cool.*
IDEMITSU MUSEUM OF ARTS, TOKYO, JAPAN.

Yosa Buson (1716-1784): *Night Snow over City* (detail).
HARUTA MUTO, KŌBE, JAPAN.

V   Buson's night scene
wakes up

the spirit of
Japan:

old dark under
new light snow (now

modern cities
get it

in fine
ridges along

the phone
lines).

Sesshū (1420-1506): *Autumn and Winter Landscapes* (Autumn).
TOKYO NATIONAL MUSEUM, TOKYO, JAPAN.

VI   Every
thing

lives. This
is

Sesshū's
gift.

Strokes flash
black

branch out
fade.

Zigzag
rocks

knuckled
twigs

reeds
bowing

bowing
monks

face
to face

on stone
stairs:

one
who walks

has
a face;

others
live

without
one.

This world
looks

made
to live

for

ever.

That's why
we

turn
to it—

a lie
five

centuries
old.

It's
autumn.

Winter
comes

once
again

cold
water.

Leaves
fall and

temple
roofs

stick out
stark

jagged
rocks

lives
mindful

of this
cold

mountain
stream

where they've
stepped.

VII   But in this name,
      "Empty White House," hope
    Dawns, flowers bloom,
    Burns's flake of snow
    Falls. It is home,
    Sengai's no abode

    Where evanishing's
    A coming home
    That makes us love things
    On the way, "skim-
    Ming bare trees" on wings
    Or skimming cream.

    Sengai retired
    At *Kyo Haku In*.
    He sat, prepared
    His paper and ink,
    Painted a bird,
    A flower, a tree.

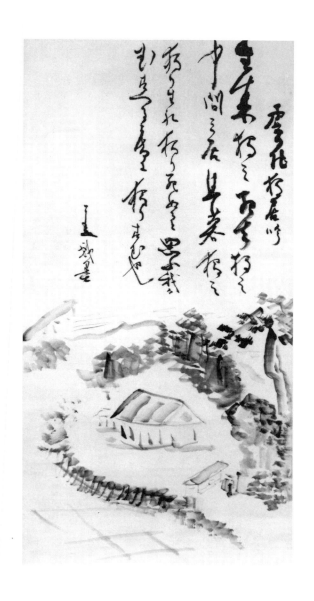

Sengai (1751-1837): *Solitary Life at Kyohaku-in*.
IDEMITSU MUSEUM OF ARTS, TOKYO, JAPAN.

Shih K'o (10th century): *Second Patriarch Harmonizing His Mind.*
TOKYO NATIONAL MUSEUM, TOKYO, JAPAN.

VIII Master! Whose
master? Of what?

Second Patriarch,
they say,

and "harmonizing his
mind."

When names become
all to us

we see nothing
with our eyes:

that he has a gut
and tilts

crutched
on a bony elbow;

ringed wrist, too limp
to hold up

his head,
gives way, gaunt hand slips

on the stubble
of his chin,

and in dishabille
he nods;

unmuscled, weak-lunged,
no good

to rice paddy or
women.

But what does
he have in mind,

just to sit
for centuries

on his ass?
Ah, here's the danger—

either way to doubt.
Master,

oh emptier of
bottles,

slumped world eraser
smoothing

those deep wrinkles
in your brain,

let me not doubt you!
I know

the sea breeze
ruffling your sleeve

can't touch your thoughts of
nothing.

X   After a month of reading
Li Po and Tu Fu,
A vivid picture holds fast:
Ming-huang's flight to Shu
On the cover of the book,
An old Chinese scene
Of high pines, long clouds winding
Between peaks, still green
After centuries of thrones
Overthrown, regained
And lost again, the trees still
In leaf, nothing's waned,
The Glorious Emperor
Himself remains fresh
As the low plain where he rides
Which blends with his flesh.
Through a saddle in the ridge
Far hills die toward
A shoreless lake where, in time,
All fall overboard.
But the path Ming-huang travels!
The fantastic trace
Of mere scantlings trussed on piles
High up the rock face
Of a pinnacle—it's this
Matchless mastery
That holds me, here, where trees leaf,
Streams flow, and men flee—
It's this presence of beauty
Indifferent to who,
Among many escaping,
Are the retinue
And who China's apogee,
Ming-huang—this jade rock,
Tree-topped, leaning, looking down
Like a stony hawk.

Anonymus (T'ANG DYNASTY, 618-906):
Emperor Ming-huang's Journey to Shu.
NATIONAL PALACE MUSEUM, TAIPEI, TAIWAN, REPUBLIC OF CHINA.

XI   Here you are again, Governor,
on your lean donkey
shuffling through an emptiness
you filled with new thoughts
like crows in winter fir trees
shaking off the snow.
Pien Luan's sparrows live
like you on paper,
a thousand years, one more day.
Effortless, simple.
The vast white space around you
contains every bird,
every pine and jujube tree,
the soft hiss of rain,
friends arriving with clear wine,
the clatter of hoofs
outside, smoke in the cool air.
And now a jet's whine
sharp as a shrill cicada:
Does it pierce your dream,
Su Tung-p'o? What do you dream
as you drift, nodding,
but a shadow on the snow?

Ogata Kōrin (1658-1716): *Su Tung-p'o Riding a Donkey*.

Sesshū (1420-1506): *Larger Landscape Scroll* (detail).
Mōri Mtotaka, Hōfu, Tatara, Japan.

Apartments packed close,
set at odd angles, some low
at the river's edge,
some overlooking neighbors;
the mountains behind
echo the roofs' jagged lines;
tiles, thatch, plain white walls,
here and there latticed windows...
with electric wires
strung from poles to weatherheads
it could be today
somewhere along Japan's coast.
Sesshū painted it
as he saw it, and it lives.
In a high window
someone's threading a needle
or maybe blowing
her nails while she daydreams
of a better life.
I looked up from my walk in
Hiratsuka as
she thumbed through a magazine,
just three years ago!
And men drying nets on boats
or cleaning their catch,
how are they different from men
now docked in Itō?
Reeds and rocks screen the houses
as they did before
ink and brush came to Japan.
Everywhere the same:
at Palazzo Tolornia
the seamed marble face
of that old Roman shows what
small alteration
two thousand years make in man.
Pine trees fade in mist,
waves lap against hulls, two heads
just over the reeds
face one another, and talk.

Ku K'ai-chih (344-405), attribution: *Admonitions of the Court Instructress.*
BRITISH MUSEUM, LONDON.

XIII   In the oldest scroll painting
        we find Ku K'ai-chih

        lost in his subject,
        the life of man and woman.

        Sixteen hundred years man's perched,
        his slippers half off,

        at the edge of her
        canopied bed, uncertain.

        That face of his makes me tired!
        What do you expect

        to see, sir, behind
        those laquered eyes, black as night?

        This silk-robed aristocrat
        could be Sleepy John

        bending a steel string
        ("Mama, won't you stop that thing")

        but for his courtly rearing.
        However refined

        he looks unwilling
        to break free from his bondage.

        The woman grips her hinged screen
        and returns his stare,

        defiant, sitting
        straight, her head level with his.

        What she has said, what he heard
        to plant that distrust

        in him, we all know.
        It still puts an edge on eyes

        like hers. It tenses our lips.
        We paint it, sing it.

        When it stops, life stops,
        reverberation of life.

Ku K'ai-chih (344-405), attribution: *Admonitions of the Court Instructress.*
BRITISH MUSEUM, LONDON.

XIV Another scene shows the man
holding up his hand

to say, "Stop, woman!"
as he turns away from her.

Disclosing his cold reproach
the lady's silk scarves

blow back. That's his mind
speaking a wind cold as ice.

Does her beauty not hold him:
her hand in her sleeve

raised before her breast,
the fine black eyebrows lifted

in frank astonishment? "What
have I done? Tell me!"

How can he tell her?
Whose skin's more like silk than hers,

whose supple figure more straight?
His bearing can't hide

the man who can't speak
his heart, that hardness but glass

through which we see her beauty
blaze up in his veins.

Love, here is your slave,
half-returned before he goes.

XV   When the summer evening's cool,
enjoy it. Bamboo
stops shooting up through clotheslines,
cicadas calm down,
Venus holds an edge.

Kusumi Morikage's
peasant family
have their mat spread out under
a calabash vine
and want nothing more.

All three in light summer robes
look one way, content.
Moonlight drops through the broad leaves
and spreads out its silk,
day's warmth in the ground.

Mother, child, father, silent.
What's to talk about?
The hill or lake they look at
comes through thinner mist.
What's to see beyond?

The grass roof tells us they're poor,
but what does that mean
tonight? The man's muscled arms
loosen, the cool moon
touches his wife's hands.

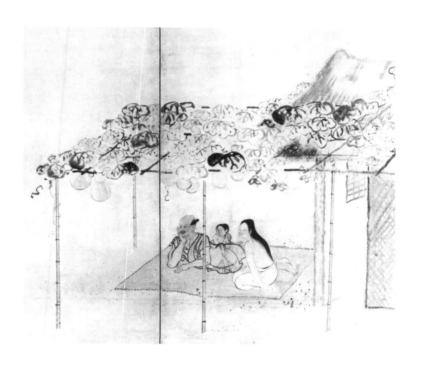

Kusumi Morikage (ca. 1610-ca. 1700): *Enjoying the Evening Cool.*
TOKYO NATIONAL MUSEUM, TOKYO, JAPAN.

Mu-ch'i (fl.mid-13th century): *Persimmons.*
RYŌKŌIN, DAITOKUJI, KYŌTO, JAPAN.

XVI   Mu-ch'i's six persimmons
were all he had in mind
when his brush touched the ink.
Who has words stark enough
to keep out all but them?
Their overwhelming calm

has no resting place, not
so much as a table.
But to disturb them is
unimaginable.
Each persimmon varies
yet all six are one fruit.

The stems dance on one toe.
Two faint moonlike crescents
of fruit flank the row, gapped
where one is out of line.
Waned, they are persimmons
no less than the full one

at center. As soon as
I think, this might stand for
the mystery of life,
it's just a persimmon,
squat, dark, squarish—shaped like
a television screen.

An old tree in winter
beside a tennis court
accented students' shouts.
But those few persimmons
bright against a blue sky
cannot explain Mu-ch'i's,

broken off their branches,
untouched with orange. These
can't be sliced into stars
and eaten with the eyes.
Who see his persimmons
as they are are as they.

灌園便

築成小圃近方塘菓易生成菜易長也雍太少

撥太巧匡中酌取逢園方

Ike Taiga (1723-1776): *The Convenience of Gardening.*
KAWABATA YASUNARI FOUNDATION, KAMAKURA, JAPAN.

XVII   Convenience, comfort—
do these words fit

having to dig up
the sour grass,

turn compacted clay,
sow, and stand in

invading nature's way?
Kids trample

the new corn, heat wilts
leaves fog mildews

and squash comes full tilt.
Soon we sicken

of its taste.
Love grew in a garden,

and there's the real thing:
manure and string.

Was Leonidas
just wishing, then?

"Here's Klito's little
shack, his little

cornpatch, his tiny
vineyard, his little

woodlot. Here Klito
spent eighty years."

How diminutively
lovely his

life
cultivated by poetry.

Am I missing something:
how to hoe

and smile happily
over eggplant,

come what may
sweet on a sprawling vine?

No hours in
Taiga's farmer's day,

no weight in the water
he pours, no,

this life's sprung free
below a blue tree

in a green field,
loose as an old fence.

XVIII   I see
          the quiet

          in winter,
          a tree

          sheltering
          two crows

          (god-blackened
          shadows

       "clatter no more
          o'er

          fishermen's
          lanthorns").

          I'm as good as
          there

          with them
          just downbranch

          where its white
          widens

          and the crows
          rivet

          their brassy eyes
          to

          mine.
       "Who comes here now

          a hundred
          thousand

          dusks have passed?"
          Silence.

Yosa Buson (1716-1784): *Crows* (detail).
KITAMURA MUSEUM, KYŌTO, JAPAN.

Flakes of snow
like flakes

of light
between leaves

make a night
of stars

now,
now there's no *gnaw*

gnaw of crows,
just two

still crows still
at rest.

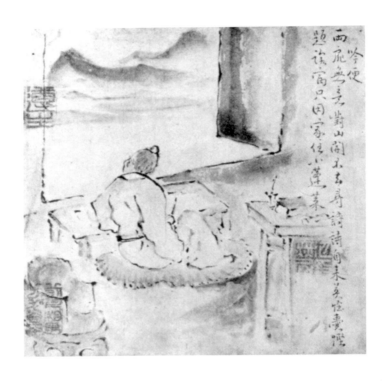

吟便
兩一庭無事對山閒不去尋詩
詩自來矣住雲邊
題後窗只因家後小蓬萊心

Ike Taiga (1723-1776): *The Convenience of Reciting Poetry.*
Kawabata Yasunari Foundation, Kamakura, Japan.

XIX   Flutters away
then turns

back again
and again

flutters, pauses
and turns

like the flute player's
trill

in "Crane's Brooding":
the thought

a poet looks
at out through

his window
and feels, feels

now a mountain
now mind

elusively
moving.

Anonymous (late Ming Dynasty, 1368-1644): *Asleep in a Boat near the Shore.*
FREER GALLERY OF ART, SMITHSONIAN INSTITUTION, WASHINGTON, D.C.

XX   When hungry, eat;
thirsty, drink.

You can't sleep
pulled at like that,

boat moored
to a log on shore.

Sparrows *chup chup*
on rice stalks,

waves slap, wheels
chatter, hoofs rap.

Two ducks fly away
the way

wind blows
bamboo over you,

a black splash
(shadow?) hurtles

without a thought
off a rock,

an invisible
current

beckons
you and your thin oar.

Go.
Cut the line. Lake and sky

alike. Light,
mist all around.

Others
have drifted there before.